Destination Detectives

India

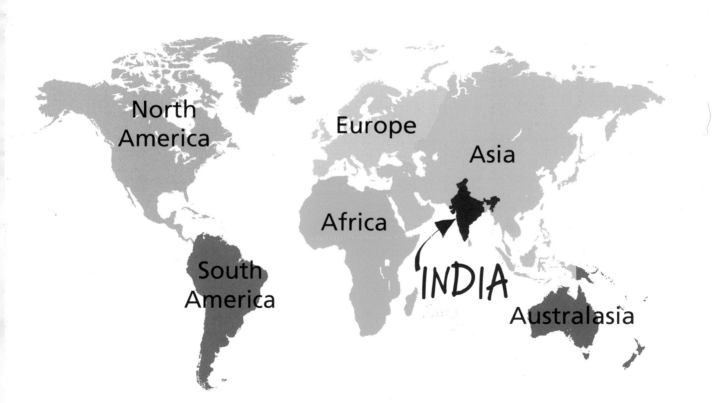

North America

Europe

Asia

Africa

South America

INDIA

Australasia

Anita Roy

www.raintreepublishers.co.uk
Visit our website to find out more information about **Raintree** books.

To order:
 Phone 44 (0) 1865 888112
 Send a fax to 44 (0) 1865 314091
Visit the Raintree Bookshop at **www.raintreepublishers.co.uk** to browse our catalogue and order online.

First published in Great Britain by Raintree,
Halley Court, Jordan Hill, Oxford OX2 8EJ,
part of Harcourt Education.
Raintree is a registered trademark of Harcourt
Education Ltd.

Editorial: Melanie Copland and Lucy Beevor
Design: Victoria Bevan and Kamae Design
Picture Research: Hannah Taylor and Kay Altwegg
Production: Duncan Gilbert

Originated by Dot Gradations
Printed and bound in China
by WKT Company Limited

ISBN-10: 1 844 2140 60 (hardback)
ISBN-13: 978 1 844 2140 68 (hardback)
10 09 08 07 06
10 9 8 7 6 5 4 3 2 1

ISBN-10: 1 844 2144 19 (paperback)
ISBN-13: 978 1 844 2144 19 (paperback)
11 10 09 08 07 06
10 9 8 7 6 5 4 3 2 1

British Library Cataloguing in Publication Data
Roy, Anita
India. – (Destination Detectives)
954'.0531
A full catalogue record for this book is available from
the British Library.

Acknowledgements
Alamy Images pp. 32 (Barend Gerr), 29 (david sanger
photography), 20 (dubassy), 12–13 (easywind), 24–25 (Fabrice
Bettex), 19l (Fiona Jeffrey), 23t (Helene Rogers), 4–5 (PCL),
28r (Peter Adams Photography); Bridgeman Art Library p. 19r;
Corbis pp. 43 (Adam Woolfitt), 21 (Angelo Hornak), 36
(Catherine Karnow), 39 (David Samuel Robbins), pp. 23b, 40l
(Earl & Nazima Kowall), 42l (Elio Ciol), 16 (Enzo & Paolo
Ragazzini), 18 (Gian Berto Vanni), pp. 9, 10–11, 27, 34–35,
40r (Jeremy Horner), 6t (Jim Zuckerman), pp. 6bl, 24, 41
(Lindsay Hebberd), pp. 22, 6br (Reuters), 37 (Reuters/Arko
Datta), 38 (Reuters/Javanta Shaw), 34 (Ted Streshinsky);
Corbis Royalty Free 17l; Getty Images pp. 25 (AFP), pp. 17r,
42r (Photodisc), Harcourt Education Ltd pp. 13, 15, 33l, 33r
(Rob Bowden/ EASI-Images), 28l (Sharron Lovell); Magnum
Photos p. 14 (Ian Berry); Panos Pictures p. 11 (Karen
Robinson), pp. 5, 31 (Mark Henley); Photolibrary.com p. 26;
Rex Features p. 12; Robert Harding pp. 8–9 (Sybil Sassoon).

Cover photograph of of brightly coloured spices reproduced
with permission of Getty/Photodisc.

Every effort has been made to contact copyright
holders of any material reproduced in this book.
Any omissions will be rectified in subsequent
printings if notice is given to the publishers.

The paper used to print this book comes from
sustainable resources.

Contents

Any words appearing in the text in bold, **like this,** are explained in the glossary. You can also look out for them in the Word Bank box at the bottom of each page.

India at your doorstep

In most Indian cities and towns, people buy their daily supplies from people pushing carts along the road. These handcarts are piled high with fresh fruit and vegetables, buckets and mops, and even carpets! The cry of the *sabji-wallah* (vegetable seller) is a familiar sound throughout India.

You wake up to the sound of a vegetable seller shouting "*Sabji!*" Sparrows twitter, parakeets screech. The sun is shining and the air is breezy, but warm. As you step outside, a group of children covered in paint and carrying water pistols runs up to you.

"Happy Holi!" they yell, and suddenly throw a fistful of coloured powder paint at you. It's the spring festival of Holi, where everyone goes a little crazy – throwing water balloons, dancing in the streets, smearing each other with paint, and generally having fun. It's a wet, wild, and colourful welcome to India!

The spring festival of Holi, or the "festival of colours", celebrates the end of winter and the beginning of springtime.
▶

WORD BANK   empire group of countries controlled by one country

Indians make up nearly one-sixth of the world's population – that's over a billion people! It's a huge country to explore, and what better place to start than from the capital city: Delhi?

Which direction will you take? Will you go:
- north to the snow-capped mountains of the Himalayas?
- west to see the camels and historical forts of Rajasthan?
- south through the forests of Madhya Pradesh and down to the **tropical** coconut groves of Kerala?
- east to explore rural Bengal and the busy former capital of Kolkata (Calcutta)?

A tale of two cities

Delhi is actually two cities in one. Old Delhi, with its winding alleys, dates back to 1638. The British built New Delhi to be the capital city in the early 1900s. At that time India was part of the British **Empire**.

The Rashptrapati Bhavan – the president's house – in Delhi.

tropical climate near to Earth's equator where it is humid and warm all year round

A varied land

The "Seven Sisters"

The seven states in north-eastern India contain some of the wildest and most beautiful mountains and forests in the country. Relatively cut off from the rest of India, most of the people in these states are from different tribes, each with its own customs, and styles of dress. There are over twenty languages spoken in this region alone!

On the pavement outside, a man is selling poster-size maps of India. You buy one for a few rupees (Indian coins). The first thing you realize is that India is huge! You could get the whole of the UK into it thirteen times! There are mountains and **plains**, rivers and beaches, hills and deserts. You need to decide which place to visit first, so you know whether to pack warm sweaters or cool T-shirts. You read your guidebook and begin to add labels to the map to help you decide.

These women wear heavily embroidered ghagra (skirts) and choli (blouses), decorated with tiny mirrors that sparkle in the sunlight.

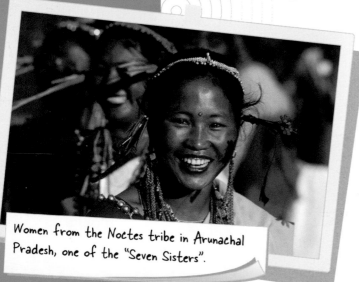

Women from the Noctes tribe in Arunachal Pradesh, one of the "Seven Sisters".

Using water from the Sutlej and Beas Rivers, the soil of Punjab is good farming land. Most people who live here are Sikhs.

WORD BANK plain large, flat area of land

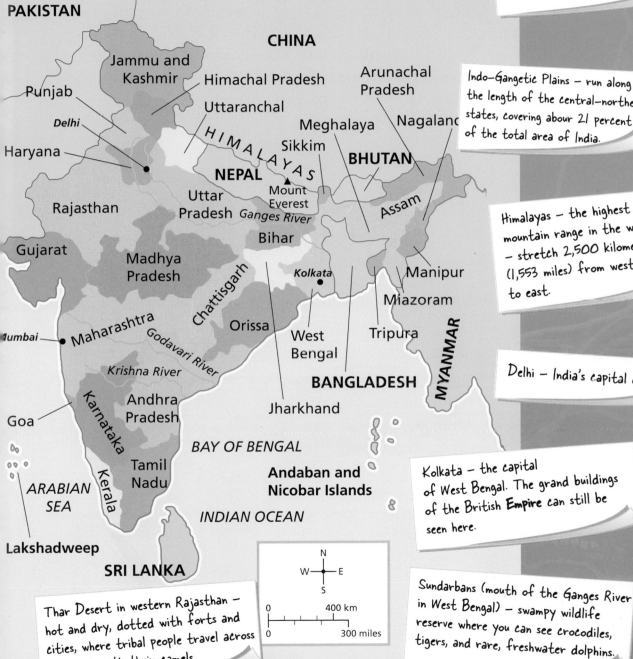

Mumbai (Bombay) — one of the most densely populated areas in the world and home to India's Hindi film industry, known by many as "Bollywood". It is famous for its Portuguese cathedrals and beautiful beaches and is a favourite for winter holidaymakers in search of sunshine.

Jammu and Kashmir — tourists have to get special permission to travel here because of disputes between India and Pakistan over this territory.

Indo-Gangetic Plains — run along the length of the central-northern states, covering abour 21 percent of the total area of India.

Himalayas — the highest mountain range in the world — stretch 2,500 kilometres (1,553 miles) from west to east.

Delhi — India's capital city.

Kolkata — the capital of West Bengal. The grand buildings of the British **Empire** can still be seen here.

Sundarbans (mouth of the Ganges River in West Bengal) — swampy wildlife reserve where you can see crocodiles, tigers, and rare, freshwater dolphins.

Thar Desert in western Rajasthan — hot and dry, dotted with forts and cities, where tribal people travel across the sands with their camels.

PAKISTAN
CHINA
Jammu and Kashmir
Himachal Pradesh
Punjab
Uttaranchal
Delhi
Arunachal Pradesh
Meghalaya
Nagaland
H I M A L A Y A S
Sikkim
BHUTAN
Haryana
NEPAL
Mount Everest
Rajasthan
Uttar Pradesh
Ganges River
Assam
Gujarat
Bihar
Madhya Pradesh
Kolkata
Chattisgarh
Manipur
Miazoram
Maharashtra
Godavari River
Orissa
West Bengal
Tripura
MYANMAR
Krishna River
Andhra Pradesh
BANGLADESH
Goa
Karnataka
Jharkhand
Mumbai
BAY OF BENGAL
Kerala
Tamil Nadu
Andaban and Nicobar Islands
ARABIAN SEA
INDIAN OCEAN
Lakshadweep
SRI LANKA

N
W   E
S

0   400 km
0   300 miles

Geography

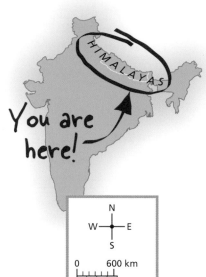

You are here!

N
W — E
S

0   600 km
0   400 miles

It's beginning to get hot in Delhi, so you decide to head for the hills. After 5 hours of driving across flat **plains,** you can see the **foothills** in the distance. The air gets cooler as the road zigzags up. Monkeys sitting at the side of the road watch as you drive past. The views are spectacular. There are forests and waterfalls, and in the far distance you glimpse the snow-capped peaks of the Himalayan mountains.

Hill stations

The Himalayan foothills have many pretty villages and small towns, such as Darjeeling and Simla. The British rulers made their summer homes in these **hill stations** in the 1900s. It is strange to see such British-looking bungalows and churches right here in India!

The Darjeeling Himalayan Railway first started running in 1881. It's so slow that you can even hop off on one bend and walk to catch it up at the next.

WORD BANK   foothills lower slopes of mountains

The Himalayas include some of the highest peaks on Earth: Kanchenjunga, K2, and Mount Everest. The mountains form a barrier separating northern India from its neighbours. The Himalayas are the world's youngest mountains as well as the highest – and they're still growing! Recent discoveries suggest that they're growing upwards at about 6.1 centimetres (2.4 inches) per year.

The Himalayas are **sacred** mountains to many Indians. You can see Hindu temples and shrines everywhere. In Ladakh and Sikkim, you see Buddhist prayer flags fluttering on poles. The air here is so clear and the views so stunning, it's no wonder people think that it is "Heaven on Earth".

The five treasures of the snow

The highest mountain in the Indian Himalayas is Kanchenjunga. Its name comes from the Tibetan words, *kanchen* and *dzonga* meaning "five treasures of the great snow".

Highest mountains in the world
Mount Everest (Nepal): 8,850 metres (29,034 feet)
K2 (Pakistan): 8,611 metres (28,250 feet)
Kanchenjunga (Nepal-India): 8,586 metres (28,169 feet)

sacred to do with religion or worship

To tap the energy of India's rivers, the government has built huge dams to generate **hydroelectricity**. Over 3,300 big dams have been built, generating about 17 percent of India's electricity, and making India the world's third largest dam builder.

Rivers

As you travel through the mountains, you see rivers cutting their way through **gorges**. Where two rivers meet, there are often temples to mark them as **sacred** spots. Many of India's rivers start from the Himalayas including:

- the Brahmaputra
- the Indus
- the Yamuna
- the mighty Ganges, the most sacred river of all, or *Ma Ganga* as it is called in India.

The Ganges starts its 2,506 kilometre- (1,557 mile-) long journey high up in an ice cave on the southern slopes of the Himalayas. From there it flows down to the **plains**, and winds towards the eastern coast. There it joins with the Brahmaputra and empties into the Bay of Bengal.

Women gather on the banks of the Ganges to wash and offer prayers to *Ma Ganga*, the most sacred of all rivers. ➤

WORD BANK   gorge   deep, narrow valley between hills
hydroelectricity   electricity produced by the flow of water

All along the banks of the Ganges, you'll see people washing clothes, bathing, and often praying or meditating. The ancient city of Varanasi (also known as Benares) has *ghats* (steps) leading down to the water. Priests and **pilgrims** gather here to offer their prayers, especially at dawn and sunset. The water of the Ganges is sacred to Hindus and one dip in the river is supposed to wash away all sins. Many Hindus also believe that when they die, their ashes should be scattered into the Ganges.

You should think twice about taking a dip, though. The lower stretches of the Ganges are highly **polluted**, with nearly 1 billion litres (2.1 billion pints) of waste going into the river every day.

Rivers of death

Many people argue that damming rivers causes more damage than good – to people's lives and homes, and to the environment. One of India's most famous writers, Arundhati Roy, compares big dams to nuclear bombs saying, "They're both weapons of mass destruction".

Villagers cling to their homes as the waters rise all around them after a huge dam was built on the Narmada River in Madhya Pradesh.

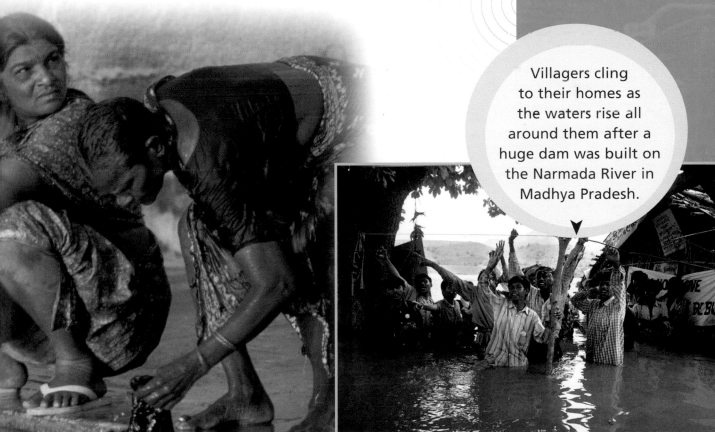

pilgrim   someone who goes on a religious journey to a sacred place
pollution   harmful waste or chemicals released into the air, water, or soil

Plains, coasts, and islands

Surrounded by mountains, you begin to wonder if all of India is like this! You find a tourist guide and ask him. He says that you need to head down through the lush Indo-Gangetic **plains** of central-northern India to the Deccan **Plateau** in the south. This plateau is dry and rocky. On either side are two sets of gentle hills. Known as the Eastern and Western *Ghats* (steps), these run alongside the coastline.

You decide to explore the beaches. You fly to Mumbai and then take the Konkan railway line. It runs along the western coast all the way down to Mangalore. From the train, you can see miles of sandy beaches, fringed with coconut palms. You can see fishing boats out at sea, and villagers drying fish and mending their nets on the beach.

▲ Whole villages were destroyed in the tsunami of December 2004.

► The Andaman Islands are famous for their paradise beaches.

India also has two sets of islands. To the west there are the coral islands of Lakshadweep. To the east there is a cluster of more than 300 islands called the Andaman and Nicobar Islands. Both sets of islands are home to many rare birds, fish, and plants. The Andamans are most famous as the breeding ground for the rare Olive Ridley sea turtles that lay their eggs here every year.

Gone fishing
The coasts of India are dotted with tiny fishing villages. Fishermen still venture out in traditional boats to bring in their daily haul of fish. Women help to sort and clean the fish, and carry them to market in wicker baskets on their heads.

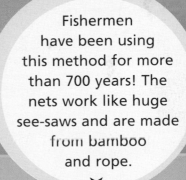

Fishermen have been using this method for more than 700 years! The nets work like huge see-saws and are made from bamboo and rope.

tsunami huge tidal wave caused by an earthquake

Climate

N
W E
S

0   600 km

0   400 miles

You are here!

Kerala

The further south you travel, the hotter and stickier it gets. As summer temperatures soar, people wait anxiously for the **monsoon** rains to start. You decide to keep heading down the coast, to meet the rains along the coast of Kerala in early June. As the storm clouds gather over the sea, and the first drops start to fall, everyone rushes out to celebrate. People dance in the streets and children splash about in puddles.

Cool it!

Most Indian homes have ceiling fans – essential for keeping cool in the hot, summer months. Before electricity, people used to hang blinds made of rushes across their windows and doors, which they would keep wetting with water to keep them cool.

► Children of the village of Cherrapunji, the wettest place on Earth, dance with joy to welcome the heavy monsoon rains.

WORD BANK   monsoon rainy season, from June to August

The monsoon travels north up the country in June and July, bringing much-needed rain. During the monsoon months, 80 percent of the year's rainfall happens. For farmers, a good monsoon means a healthy crop. A bad one can mean **starvation**.

India has a lot of different weather! It has the wettest place in the world – in the north-east – and also one of the driest. While the rest of India is drenched by the monsoon rains, hardly a drop falls on the Great Thar Desert in western Rajasthan. Here, in the summer, the daytime temperature can climb to a sizzling 50 °C (120 °F).

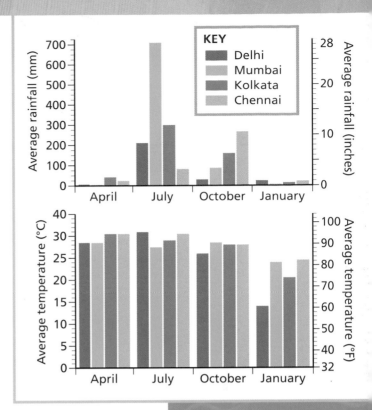

Even in the driest, hottest areas of India, farmers grow crops and work the land.

starvation lack of basic food needed to survive

Wildlife

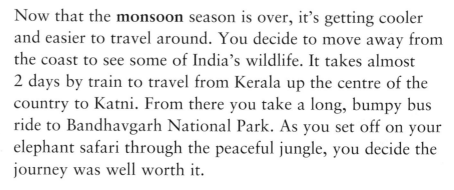

Elephant workers

Did you know that some employees of the Indian government are animals? Indian elephants are still used to carry mail to remote parts of the country. They even get pensions once they are too old to work!

Now that the **monsoon** season is over, it's getting cooler and easier to travel around. You decide to move away from the coast to see some of India's wildlife. It takes almost 2 days by train to travel from Kerala up the centre of the country to Katni. From there you take a long, bumpy bus ride to Bandhavgarh National Park. As you set off on your elephant safari through the peaceful jungle, you decide the journey was well worth it.

High up in the thick forest trees you can see monkeys clambering about in search of food. Pointing to the ground, the *mahout* (elephant driver) shows you where an animal has left tracks in the mud. "Too small for a tiger," he says. "Maybe a leopard or jungle cat." A little further on, the elephant suddenly freezes. The sambar deer in the forest put up their heads, ready to run. Then you hear it – the spine-chilling roar of a tiger near by.

India used to have thousands of tigers, but now there are only a few hundred left. Many have been lost to **poaching** and hunting. Huge areas of their natural **habitat** have been taken over by humans. To protect this wonderful animal, national parks and **sanctuaries**, such as Bandhavgarh, have been set up.

WORD BANK   habitat   place where animals live
poaching   illegal hunting of wild animals

Tigers will become extinct in the wild unless their habitat is protected.

The sacred snake

Snakes are thought to be **sacred** animals by Hindus, and many Hindu gods are always pictured with snakes. There is even a festival where people offer milk, honey, and flowers to cobras and other snakes.

sanctuary in the case of animals, a safe place for them to live where they are protected from poachers and life-threatening changes to their habitat

India is one of the world's oldest civilizations – there were cities along the Indus Valley over 4,000 years ago! As you travel around, try to imagine what life was like hundreds or thousands of years ago.

Mauryan Empire

Pilgrims from all over the world come to visit the oldest Buddhist site in the world, Sanchi in central India. As you stand in front of the huge, stone-carved gateway, you can see the three-headed lions that were the symbol of the ruler of the Mauryan **Empire**, King Ashoka. The lions became India's official **emblem** and are also shown on the back of the rupee coin.

British Empire

The British ruled India for almost 200 years. This period was known as the British Raj. The Raj was at its most powerful during the reign of Queen Victoria (1837–1901). During this time, the British ruled nearly a quarter of the world's population, and India was called "the jewel in the Empire's crown".

Gateway of India

The Gateway of India in Mumbai was built by the British to last as long as the British Empire – forever! But this huge sandstone archway was finished in 1924 – just 23 years before the British left and India became an **independent** country.

The Gateway of India is Mumbai's most famous monument.

Vijayanagara Empire

Further south, the ancient city of Hampi was at the heart of one of the greatest Hindu kingdoms in Indian history, the Vijayanagara Empire. When the city was conquered in 1565, it took hundreds of elephants more than 6 months to carry away all its treasures!

Mughal Empire

There is lots to learn about the rise and fall of the Mughal Empire in Agra. If you climb up the tower at Agra Fort, you can gaze across the Yamuna River to the magnificent Taj Mahal. This was set up by the Mughal Emperor, Shah Jahan (see picture below), as a **monument** to his dead wife. It took 22 years to build.

This is the Narasimha shrine in Hampi. It was carved from a single boulder!

independent when a country is ruled by its own people rather than a foreign power

Hindu gods

Hindus believe in reincarnation – which means that after you die, your soul is reborn in another body. Good deeds in this life count towards a good next life, and vice versa. This is known as karma. You'll be amazed at how many Hindu gods and goddesses there are! The main ones are:

Brahma – the creator

Vishnu – the preserver

Shiva – the destroyer.

Religion

You soon find out that religion, for most Indians, is very important. Religion is who you are, your culture, your surroundings, and your daily life. There are many different religions in India, as the pie chart on the right shows.

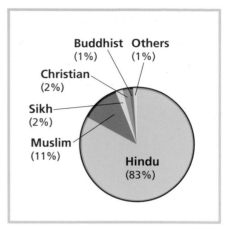

Buddhist (1%) Others (1%)
Christian (2%)
Sikh (2%)
Muslim (11%)
Hindu (83%)

➤ Hindu *mandirs* (temples) are dedicated to one or other of the gods and goddesses and usually have a large statue of them. Shiva, the destroyer, sits in the Chattapur *mandir* in New Delhi.

Hinduism

Step into an ordinary Hindu house, and you'll see gods everywhere – in paintings, on calendars, and as little statues. In the corner of one room, you'll often find a small shrine decorated with flowers and incense sticks.

Hindu prayer **rituals** are called *poojas*. They are performed at all major ceremonies – at weddings, for newly born babies, and at funerals, too. Often, people do small *poojas* as part of their daily routine. They burn incense, offer flowers, and chant prayers. Sometimes a bell is struck or a conch shell is blown to mark the beginning and end of the *pooja*.

Elephant-headed Ganesh

Parvati, wife of the Hindu god Shiva, had a son called Ganesh. One day Shiva cut off Ganesh's head in a fit of rage. Then Shiva brought him back to life by putting an elephant's head on his shoulders. Ganesh is thought to bring good fortune to his worshippers.

Parvati, the mother of Ganesh, also appeared as the dreaded goddess Kali, and performed a "dance of destruction". Here, she dances on the corpse of one of her victims.

Zoroastrianism

Indian Zoroastrians are called Parsis. Most of them live in Maharashtra. They believe that fire is sacred, and are followers of the ancient prophet Zoroaster. One of the most famous Parsis was the late Freddie Mercury, lead-singer of the rock band Queen.

Islam

Islam is the second biggest religion in India. Although Muslims make up only 11 percent of the population, India has the second-largest number of Muslims of any country in the world. Muslims believe in one god, Allah, and that his **prophet** was Muhammad. If you listen at the right times of day, you can often hear the *azan* – this is the call to prayer that the *muezzin* cries out from the **mosque**, often with the help of loudspeakers!

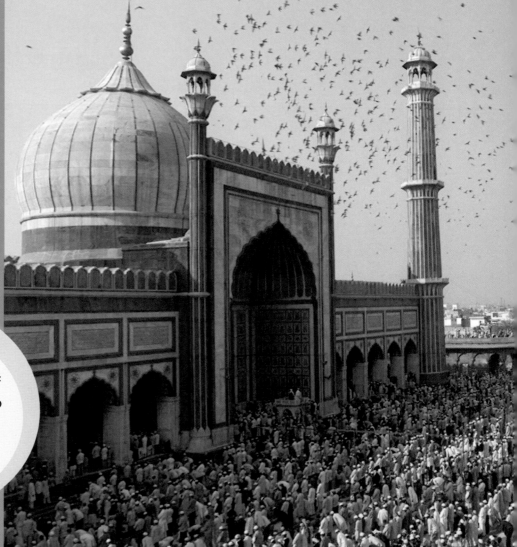

Five times a day, thousands of Muslims gather to pray at the Jama Masjid in Delhi, India's largest mosque.

muezzin   Muslim official who calls the faithful to prayer at the mosque
patron saint saint who is believed to protect a place, job, or activity

Guru Nanak was the first of ten gurus (religious teachers) to found the Sikh religion. You can see his picture in many Sikh homes, surrounded by flowers.

Buddhism

The founder of Buddhism, Siddhartha Gautama, was born in Nepal, but spent most of his life (563–483 BC) in India. Many **pilgrims** come to visit the sacred tree at Bodh Gaya in Bihar. He sat there for 49 days and became the Buddha, "The Enlightened One".

Sikhism

Sikhs make up a small percentage of India's population. You can recognize Sikh men by their turbans and beards. Most Sikhs are from the state of Punjab. Their **sacred** book is called the *Guru Granth Sahib*. It was written by Guru Nanak, the founder of the Sikh religion, and the other nine gurus. If you enter a Sikh *gurdwara* (temple), remember to cover your head, and take off your shoes as a sign of respect.

You can see many young monks at the ancient Buddhist temples throughout Ladakh.

Christianity

Most Indian Christians live in the southern states of Kerala and Goa. If you visit the Basilica of Bom Jesus in Old Goa, you can see the preserved body of Goa's **patron saint**, St Francis Xavier. The Portuguese ruled Goa for many centuries and they built this beautiful church at the start of the 17th century.

prophet person chosen by a god to communicate that god's will on Earth

Festival fur

Gods and demons

In northern India, the Dussehra festival lasts for 10 days. People celebrate the victory of the god Rama over the ten-headed demon king Ravana. On the last day, huge models of Ravana and his brothers are set on fire (below).

As you travel around the country, you soon realize that hardly a day goes by without some religious festival happening. These are often connected with the changing of the seasons, such as the harvest festival of Pongal in south India. In this festival people decorate their cows with flowers and paint their horns bright colours! Another spring festival is Holi. During this you are likely to get splattered with powder paints and bombed with water-filled balloons.

Eid is the main Muslim festival. It is celebrated after a month-long **fast**, known as Ramadan (or Ramzan). During Ramadan, Muslims are not allowed to eat after sunrise or before sunset. The last day of Ramadan is an occasion for great celebration – and lots of fabulous food!

Huge displays of fireworks and lights make up Divali, the Hindu festival of light.

WORD BANK   fast period where what you eat is very restricted

You arrive back in Delhi just in time for the biggest festival of the year: Diwali. People spend the day decorating their houses with fairy lights, candles, and little butter-lamps called *diyas*. Then, as the sun begins to set, the fireworks start. The lights and candles are to welcome the goddess of wealth, Lakshmi, into all houses. The firecrackers and rockets are to scare away any evil spirits.

Make your own *rangoli*

Rangolis are colourful patterns painted on the floor during festivals. At Diwali, Hindus draw bright *rangoli* patterns to encourage the goddess of wealth, Lakshmi, into their homes. You can make your own using poster paints, coloured sand, flower petals, and a bit of imagination!

Everyday life

Finger-licking good

Eating with your hands takes a bit of practice, but it is the best way to eat a plate of Indian food. But remember, eating with your left hand is thought to be bad manners.

When you were in Kerala, you ate crispy pancakes called *dosas* and steamed rice-cakes called *idlis* along with coconut chutney. Now that you are back in northern India, you notice that the food is very different.

You decide to stop at one of the many roadside cafes, called *dhabas*, to sample some freshly-fried *parathas* (flatbreads), smothered in home-made butter (*ghee*). They are stuffed with potato, spinach, or cauliflower, with tangy pickles and cool yoghurt (*dahi*). Wash it all down with a cup of *chai* – tea boiled up with milk, sugar, cardamoms, and ginger.

A *thali* is a plate with different dishes in little bowls so you can mix and match the flavours yourself.
➤

Every small town or city in northern India has an amazing variety of savoury snacks being sold on the streets. Known as *chaat*, these snacks are served on little leaf bowls. *Gol guppas* (or *pani puri*) are hollow, crisp balls, stuffed with potato and chickpeas, and then dipped in spiced water and eaten in one go.

Indians have a very sweet tooth and no festival is complete without lots and lots of milk sweets being eaten. Choose fat, round *laddoos*; *barfi,* made with ground cashew nuts; or curly, crunchy *jalebis* freshly-fried and dripping with sugar syrup – take your pick!

A *dhaba* selling potato cakes served with mango and chilli sauce – just one of a huge variety of snacks sold on India's streets.

SHIV HANKAR   PATATO SANDWICHES   CHAT BHANDAR

Beautiful skin

On special occasions, such as weddings or festivals, you will notice lots of Indian women with dark red patterns on their hands. This is a paste of henna, which is piped on to the hands. After it has dried, it is washed off, leaving a detailed design on the skin.

What to wear

In a big city like Delhi, you notice lots of people wearing western-style clothes. But the more you travel in smaller towns and villages, the more you will notice people dressed in traditional Indian clothes. These clothes are suited to the warmer climate.

Indian women often wear *salwar kameez*, which is a loose trouser-suit worn with a flowing scarf or *chunni* draped over the shoulders. Women also wear saris. A sari is a long piece of cloth that is wound around the woman's body. It tucks into a petticoat worn underneath, then is draped over one shoulder. A short blouse, matching the pattern or colour of the sari, stops just above the waist. It looks very elegant, and once you've got the hang of tying it, it feels quite comfortable and cool.

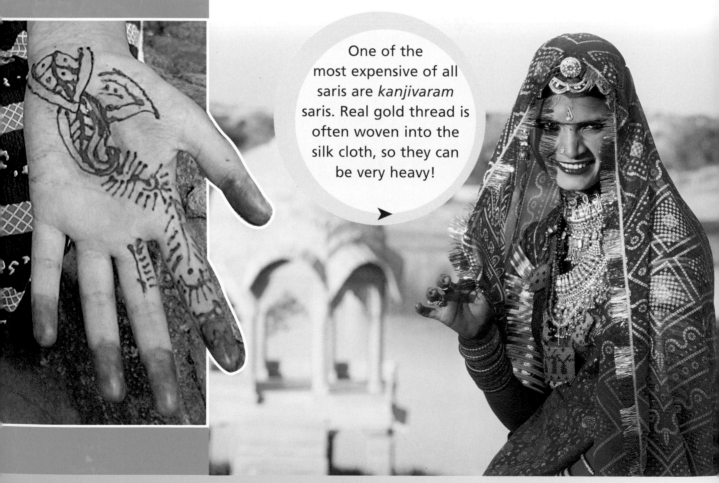

One of the most expensive of all saris are *kanjivaram* saris. Real gold thread is often woven into the silk cloth, so they can be very heavy!

You might think pyjamas are just what you wear in bed. In fact the word comes from the Indian words *pay* meaning "leg" and *jamah* meaning "clothing". Men, especially in northern India, wear loose cotton trousers called pajamas underneath long shirts called *kurtas*. In the south men usually wear a *lungi*, which is wrapped around the waist like a sarong. In Bengal men traditionally wear a *dhoti*, which is a longer length of cloth tied with drapes and folds.

Bindis

Lots of Indian women wear *bindis* – a small dot or sticker between their eyebrows. Traditionally, this was a dab of red powder, and meant that the woman was married. Today, they are often worn just because they are fun and look great.

This man from northern India wears *kurta* pyjamas, made of homespun *khadi* cotton.

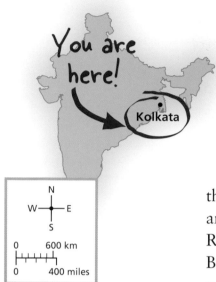

You are here!

Kolkata

Life in an Indian city

Delhi is India's capital city now, but back in the days of the British Raj Calcutta used to be the capital. You decide to take the overnight train to Kolkata, as it is now called, to see what the city is like today.

As the train pulls into Howrah station, the first thing you notice is that there are huge numbers of people. The platform is throbbing with people selling things, porters carrying luggage, beggars, travellers arriving, and travellers leaving. To cross the Hooghly River to the main city, you take a taxi across the Howrah Bridge. Two million people cross this bridge every day, making it the third-busiest bridge in the world.

City slums

Many Indian cities have large **slums**. Dhavari slum in Mumbai is the largest in Asia, housing around 1 million people. Here, there is little land space and no proper facilities such as running water or sewers. People build their makeshift houses out of any material they can find.

India has three cities in the top seven most populated cities in the world.

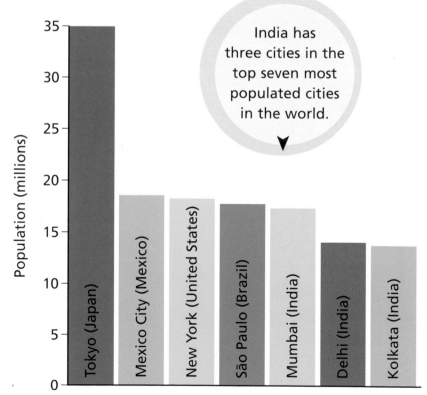

Top seven most populated cities

WORD BANK rickshaw small vehicle for carrying people and goods, either hand-pulled, pedalled, or motorised

Kolkata's streets are crowded, chaotic, and noisy. With so much traffic, air **pollution** is a big problem in all of India's cities. You can see everything on the roads from air-conditioned cars to horse-drawn carts. There are street-dogs, cows, and even the occasional elephant. Kolkata is the only city in India to still have hand-pulled **rickshaws**, as well as three-wheeled autorickshaws, and bicycle rickshaws.

All around Kolkata, you can see what used to be grand British buildings. These buildings are now in a bad state of decay because of the hot, humid climate and the air pollution.

Lunch on the move

Every day in Mumbai there are 10,000 *dabbawallahs* (delivery men) who race across the city at lunchtime. Their job is to collect *dabbas* (lunch boxes), which have been sent by workers' wives to train stations. They then deliver the *dabbas* to the workers in the city, and collect the empty boxes afterwards.

Kolkata's streets are crowded with people, traffic, and sometimes even animals!

slum area populated by very poor people, where the conditions are dirty and overcrowded

Life in an Indian village

Travel a little way out of Kolkata, and you're soon in the lush countryside of west Bengal. You see small villages with thatched huts made of mud and straw. Every village is dotted with fish ponds, because fish is an important food in Bengal.

Rural areas are home to 73 percent of all Indians. Life in an Indian village revolves around the changing seasons because villagers depend on their crops for food. After a hard day's work in the fields, villagers sit around the fire in the evening on rope-strung cots called *charpais*.

evaporate when a liquid turns into a gas or vapour and disappears

Animals are a vital part of village life. **Oxen** are used to plough the fields; cows give milk; and chickens are raised for eggs and meat. Water buffalos pull carts and also give rich, fatty milk.

People travel from village to village on bicycles, or on buffalo-carts. Life is tough here, and a good rainy season is often all that stands between survival and **starvation**. West Bengal has a rainy, damp climate so water is not such a problem. In drier areas such as Rajasthan, women have to walk for miles every day, carrying pots of water on their heads from the nearest well or pond.

A woman's work

Collecting and carrying water is seen as a woman's job. The heavy clay pots that these young women are carrying allow water to **evaporate** through the sides. This keeps the women cool on the long, hot walk back to their homes.

Buffalos and cows are very important to rural life. They give milk and are used for ploughing fields and pulling carts. Their dung is dried in the sun in flat, round cakes and used as fuel for cooking.

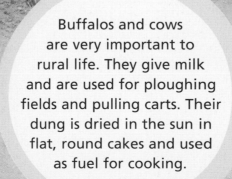

oxen male cattle

33

Travelling around India is an experience for your ears as well as your eyes! From the latest hit film-songs to religious chants, music is in the air! And where there's music, there's got to be dance, too!

The traditional dance form in Kerala is called *kathakali*. Dancers start training from a very young age to build up their strength and flexibility. The theatrical side of *kathakali* is also very important. It sometimes takes hours for the dancers to get dressed in their spectacular costumes and put on their mask-like make-up. The faces of villains are painted black, and heros are painted green. Even the eyes are tinged with a red-dye to make them stand out. A single performance can last the entire night!

On a classical note

The sitar is a long-necked instrument with up to twenty metal strings. The most famous sitar player is Pandit Ravi Shankar, whose music influenced the Beatles, one of the most famous rock bands ever. His daughters, Anoushka Shankar and Norah Jones, are now world-famous musicians, too.

Only men dance *kathakali*, so men play the female characters, too. In contrast *Bharata Natyam* is danced mainly by women. Graceful and expressive, the dancer uses her eyes, her face, and her fingers to tell a story from one of the traditional Hindu texts. Each particular movement of the hand has a different name and meaning – these are called *mudras*. The dancer wears bells around her ankles, which she jingles and stamps in time with the music.

Folk dance

Each different region of India has its own folk dances and songs. In Rajasthan, men in turbans play a one-stringed violin while the dancers twirl their multicoloured skirts to the beat of the drum. This is usually done to welcome in the new harvest season or to celebrate a wedding.

Kathakali dancers, from Kerala, in full costume and make-up.

The magic touch

A.R. Rahman is the most popular songwriter in Hindi films today. His music often helps to make a film a hit. You can hear his tunes blaring from buses, hummed along by people on the street, and even used as ringtones on mobile phones.

Hooray for Bollywood!

Every small town in India has its own cinema, and in cities there are cinemas everywhere. Indian film stars are treated almost like gods. Wherever they go to shoot a film, huge crowds gather hoping to catch a glimpse of their favourite stars.

The Indian film industry produces over 800 new releases each year. This is far, far more than the US film industry. But a big Indian blockbuster might cost US$4 million to make, while the US equivalent would cost more than US$100 million!

Huge billboards advertising the latest hit films are often painted by hand.

WORD BANK   choreographer someone who designs and arranges dances

By far the largest numbers of films are made in the Hindi language and are produced in Mumbai (Bombay). This is where the term "Bollywood" comes from. Although most of these films are in Hindi, you don't have to speak the language to enjoy the all-round entertainment of song, dance, romance, comedy, and action.

Song and dance are a vital part of all Bollywood films, after the stars and the director. The most important people are the **choreographer** and the **composer**, because no big film is complete without dance and song. Actors rarely sing. Instead they mime the songs, which are sung by professional singers. Sales of music cassettes and CDs can sometimes bring in more money than the total ticket sales at the cinema!

The most popular movie ever!

The most popular Bollywood film of all time is *Dilwale Dulhania Le Jaycage*, a romantic story of an Indian living in the United States who falls in love with an Indian girl back home. The hero is played by Shah Rukh Khan, Bollywood's biggest male star, and the movie has been running non-stop for over 10 years in Mumbai.

Hrishita Bhat (right) performs with other dancers during the shooting of the Bollywood movie *Kisna* in 2004.

composer someone who writes music

Sport and leisure

Apart from going to the cinema, Indians like to spend their free time watching cricket matches, going out to restaurants, or visiting each other's houses to chat and eat.

Cricket

Walk down any street in India and you're almost certain to see the local kids playing cricket. On the day of an important match – especially if it is India against its old rival Pakistan – the streets are empty. Everyone is following the match on television, or listening to it on the radio. Indians are cricket mad!

Indian batsman Sachin Tendulkar (right) hits a ball to boundary during the second test match against South Africa, in Kolkata, 2004.

Kabaddi

Kabbadi sport is thought to be over 4,000 years old. It is sort of like a mixture of rugby, wrestling, and tag. There are two teams of seven players each on a circular pitch. A "raider" from one team rushes to the opponent's half and tries to capture an opponent, all the while chanting "*kabaddi-kabaddi*". The trick is to get back to their half in one breath!

Carrom

On street corners you can often see groups of men playing *carrom*. This game is a bit like snooker, but played with small flat disks like draughts. Each player uses a larger disk, called the striker, to flick the other disks – black or white – into the pockets at each corner of a square board.

A group of boys play *carrom* on a street in West Bengal.

Getting out & about

Extreme India!

If you're looking for adventure, you can go white-water rafting or kayaking in the Himalayas. You can go rock climbing and trekking up its slopes, or paragliding off the peaks! You can even trek into the desert on top of a camel in Rajasthan.

If you want to really get the most out of your trip to this huge, amazing country, here's a tip . . . buses can be slow, bumpy, and uncomfortable. Travelling by plane is quick, but you miss out on all the fun of the journey. To experience the richness and variety of India, you really have to travel by train.

The British laid the first train tracks in Bombay in 1853. These soon spread across the whole country and today there are over 60,000 kilometres (37,000 miles) of track. As you travel back from Kolkata towards Delhi, you can gaze out at the changing scenery from your window. At each station, people rush through the carriage selling *chai* (tea), combs, soap, pens, peanuts, and other snacks. In the evening, you can fold the seats down to make beds.

► Men sell fresh food to passengers as their train stops at Agra Cantonment railway station, Agra, Uttar Pradesh.

Sometimes a single train journey can take several days, so it is important to be comfortable. Travelling in a group is a great way of meeting people. Indians love a good chat, and by the end of your journey, you will have made lots of friends!

If you are lucky enough to ride on the Palace of Wheels, you will be served by a waiter, eat from china plates, and drink from china teacups!

Palace on Wheels

The Palace on Wheels is a train fit for a king or queen! Starting from Delhi, you travel in ultimate luxury to Rajasthan's most famous tourist spots – the pink city of Jaipur, the lakeside splendour of Udaipur, the tiger **sanctuary** of Ranthambore, and the magnificent Taj Mahal at Agra.

The Taj Mahal

Your visit is almost over and you have to return to Delhi to catch your flight home. But before you leave, you have to visit India's most famous landmark, and one of the greatest wonders of the world – the Taj Mahal. The Mughal Emperor Shah Jahan had the Taj Mahal built in the 17th century as a **monument** to his wife Mumtaz Mahal. This incredible marble **tomb** took 22 years to complete.

Lace made of stone

The decorative screens of the Taj Mahal are carved from single, solid blocks of marble. The carvings let the light and air in, and cast shadows of beautiful patterns on the floors inside.

The Taj Mahal's gardens can be a very peaceful place to rest during a trip.

WORD BANK   tomb room where a dead body is buried

You take the morning train from Delhi to Agra, and arrive in time to spend the afternoon walking around this amazing building. The walls are inlaid with mosaics. Semi-precious stones are set into the white marble walls to make detailed designs of flowers and other patterns. It is amazing to think of the hundreds of workers who carved each petal by hand using simple chisels and hammers. The Taj is surrounded by beautiful formal gardens known as *charbagh* (four gardens).

Now you've seen the Taj Mahal, is there anything left to see? Well, plenty! You still haven't visited the Sun Temple at Konark, the ancient cave paintings at Ajanta and Ellora, or the Buddhist monasteries of Ladakh. It could take a lifetime to see all the wonders that India has to offer, and maybe your next lifetime, too.

Final resting place

Shah Jahan planned to build another Taj, entirely in black, across the river facing the Taj Mahal. But he died before it could be started, so he is buried alongside his beloved wife under the central tomb chamber of the Taj.

This is the ancient Sun Temple at Konark, built in the mid-13th century by King Narasimhadeva.

Find out more

World Wide Web

If you want to find out more about India, you can search the Internet using keywords such as these:

- India
- River Ganges
- New Delhi

You can also find your own keywords by using headings or words from this book. Try using a search directory such as **www.yahooligans.com**.

Movies

Monsoon Wedding (2002)

Directed by Mira Nair in a mixture of English and Hindi, this movie became a massive hit.

Kabhi Kushi Kabhi Gham (2001)

A great introduction to what Bollywood movies are all about. This Hindi blockbuster is packed with Bollywood's biggest stars. There's plenty to cry and laugh about, with spectacular dancing and gorgeous costumes.

Eager Destination Detectives can find out more about India using the books, websites, and addresses listed below:

The Indian Embassy

The Indian Embassy in your own country has lots of information about India. You can find out about the different regions, the best times to visit, special events, and Indian culture. Embassies in many countries have their own website. The UK embassy website address is:

www.indianembassy.co.uk

You can also write to the High Commission of India to find out more information at the following address:

High Commission of India
India House,
Aldwych,
London WC2B 4NA.

Further reading

Ancient India: People of the Ancient World, Virginia Schomp (Franklin Watts, 2005)

Cooking the Indian Way, Vijay Madavan (Lerner Publishing Company, 2003)

India: Eyewitness Guides, Manini Chatterjee and Anita Roy (Dorling Kindersley, 2002)

Lonely Planet: India, (Lonely Planet, 2003)

Rough Guide: India, (Rough Guide, 2003)

Timeline

2300 BC
People settle in
the Indus Valley.

1500–800 BC
People arrive in India
from Central Asia.

321–184 BC
Mauryan Empire spreads
across northern India.

326 BC
Greek King Alexander
the Great invades
northern India.

6th century BC
Prince Siddhartha
becomes the Buddha.

4th century AD
Gupta Empire develops
in southern India.

5–1279
Chola Empire dominates
in southern India.

1192
Mohammad Ghori
introduces Islamic rule
to northern India.

1206–1246
Mamluk (Slave) Dynasty
led by Qutb-ud-din
Aibak, a slave who
became a king; Delhi
becomes his capital city.

1216–1565
Vijayanagar Empire starts
in southern India.

1498
Portuguese explorer
Vasco Da Gama lands
in India.

1526–1707
The Mughal Empire is
at its height.

1600
British East India
Company starts
trading in India.

1632–1654
Mughal Emperor
Shah Jahan builds
the Taj Mahal.

1757
First British Governor of
Bengal, Colonel Robert
Clive, defeats the Nawab
of Bengal at the Battle
of Plassey.

1853
First steam railway sets
off from Bombay.

1857
Indian soldiers protest
against British rule;
their defeat signals the
start of the British Raj.

15 August 1947
Indian independence
declared.
Jawaharlal Nehru
becomes India's first
Prime Minister.
The country is carved
up, and Pakistan
becomes a
separate country.

1948
Mahatma Gandhi,
who led India to
independence,
is assassinated.

1965
India wars with Pakistan.

1984
Prime Minister Indira
Gandhi, Nehru's
daughter, is
assassinated by her
Sikh bodyguards.

1991
Prime Minister Rajiv
Gandhi, Indira Gandhi's
son, is assassinated.

1998
Amartya Sen wins
the Nobel Prize
for Economics.

2000
India's population
reaches 1 billion.

India – facts & figures

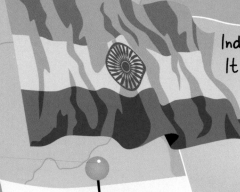

India's current flag was designed in 1947. It has three horizontal stripes – yellow, white, and green. The yellow stands for courage and sacrifice, the white is for purity, and the green is for growth. The ancient symbol in the middle is the *Dharma Chakra* (the Wheel of Law). The flag is also known as the *tiranga*, which in Hindi means "tricolour".

People and places

- Population: 1.1 billion.
- One baby is born in India every 1.25 seconds.
- India is the world's largest democracy.
- Average life expectancy: 63 years

Money matters

- The Indian railway system is the largest employer in the world, employing over 1 million people.
- According to the 2001 estimate, 25 percent of the Indian population is living in poverty.
- Average earnings: £302 (US$530)

What's in a name?

- India's name comes from the valleys around the River Indus, which were home to the early settlers.
- India's official name is Bharat Ganarajya.

Food facts

- The term "curry" isn't really used in India. There are many types of curry style dishes, which vary from region to region.
- You must only use your right hand for eating in India.
- India is the world's leading producer of mangoes.

Glossary

choreographer someone who designs and arranges dances

composer someone who writes music

emblem object used as a symbol for a place, person, or thing

empire country or group of countries ruled over by another country

evaporate when a liquid turns into a gas or vapour and disappears

fast period where what you eat is very restricted

foothills lower slopes of mountains

gorge deep, narrow valley between hills

habitat place where animals live

hill station small town in the foothills, usually built by the British when they ruled India

hydroelectricity electricity produced by the flow of water

independent when a country is ruled by its own people rather than a foreign power

monsoon rainy season, from June to August

monument building built to commemorate a major event or someone's life

mosque Muslim place of worship

muezzin Muslim official who calls the faithful to prayer at the mosque

oxen male cattle

patron saint saint who is believed to protect a place, job, or activity

pilgrim someone who goes on a religious journey to a sacred place

plain large, flat area of land

plateau area of flat land higher than the surrounding land

poaching illegal hunting to kill wild animals

pollution harmful waste or chemicals released into the air, water, or soil

prophet person chosen by a god to communicate that god's will on Earth

rickshaw small vehicle for carrying people and goods, either hand-pulled, pedalled, or motorised

ritual set of actions that are usually part of a ceremony

sacred to do with religion or worship

sanctuary in the case of animals, a safe place for them to live where they are protected from poachers and life-threatening changes to their habitat

slum area populated by very poor people, where the conditions are dirty and overcrowded

starvation lack of basic food needed to survive

tomb room where a dead body is buried

tropical climate near Earth's equator where it is humid and warm all year round

tsunami huge tidal wave caused by an earthquake

Index